for YOU

my ZIGGY FRiEND!

SIGNET Humor Books You'll Want to Read

If you wish to order these titles, please see the coupon in the back of this book.

PETS ARE FRIENDS YOU LIKE WHO LIKE YOU RIGHT BACK

ZiGGY

BY Tom Wilson

A SIGNET BOOK

NEW AMERICAN LIBRARY

TIMES MIRROR

Library of Congress Catalog Card Number: 76-52353

Published by arrangement with Sheed Andrews and McMeel, Inc.

"Ziggy" is syndicated internationally by
UNIVERSAL PRESS SYNDICATE

GOD MUST HAVE
INTENDED FOR
everyONE TO
HAVE A KITTEN

...CAUSE HE
KeePS MAKIN
SO MANY OF
THEM !!

Dear Santa,
    This may seem like a strange request, but for Christmas could you see your way clear to bring me a box of Kruncho Bisquits, ... a red ball with a bell inside, and a new chew toy

EVERY GOOD DAY BEGINS
WITH A LITTLE LOVE !!

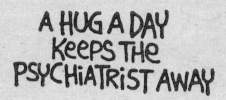

A HUG A DAY KEEPS THE PSYCHIATRIST AWAY

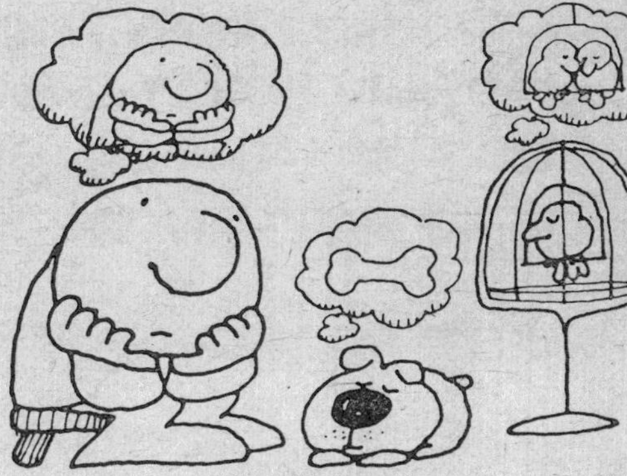

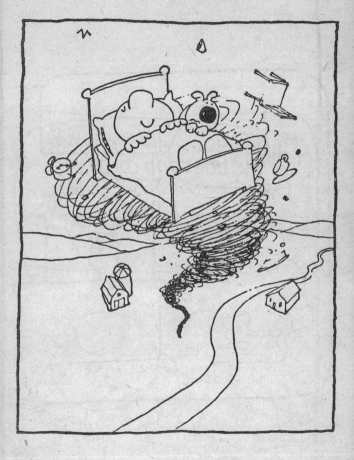

Ø

SIGNET Jumble Word Game Books by
Henri Arnold and Bob Lee

○

SIGNET Peanuts Books by Charles M. Schulz

☐ **CHARLIE BROWN'S ALL STARS** (#Y7688—$1.25)

☐ **A CHARLIE BROWN CHRISTMAS** (#Y7206—$1.25)

☐ **A CHARLIE BROWN THANKSGIVING** (#Y6885—$1.25)

☐ **IT WAS A SHORT SUMMER, CHARLIE BROWN**
(#Y7958—$1.25)

☐ **IT'S A MYSTERY, CHARLIE BROWN** (#Y8238—$1.25)

☐ **IT'S THE GREAT PUMPKIN, CHARLIE BROWN**
(#Y7809—$1.25)

☐ **PLAY IT AGAIN, CHARLIE BROWN** (#Y7344—$1.25)

☐ **THERE'S NO TIME FOR LOVE, CHARLIE BROWN**
(#Y6886—$1.25)

☐ **YOU'RE IN LOVE, CHARLIE BROWN** (#Y8175—$1.25)

☐ **YOU'RE NOT ELECTED, CHARLIE BROWN**
(#Y7016—$1.25)
